Real Lives

World War II Children

Four real children, four different lives

Sallie Purkis

Contents

A & C Black • London

Life in the Second World War

The Second World War, which lasted from 1939 until 1945, changed the lives of children around the world. Many fathers had to leave home to fight and mothers took jobs that only men had done before, such as working in factories. This happened in Britain, in countries of the British Commonwealth, in America and the Far East too.

Many British children had to leave their homes once war had broken out. They were evacuated on trains to the country and stayed with new families, where it was safer. 10,000 Jewish children from Europe came to Britain to escape from Nazi persecution. Their families sent them on special trains.

Food and clothes were rationed. Before the war, a lot of food came from abroad, but during the war the Germans began shooting the ships that carried the food. It was no longer safe for the ships to travel. This meant that there was less food and it was strictly limited.

Some children in Britain grew up without ever eating a banana and most made do with very few treats, such as sweets and cakes.

To have more food, everyone followed government advice to 'Dig for Victory' and grew their own. Most people dug up their flowerbeds and turned them into vegetable patches. Fields became allotments. At weekends the whole family would go out to tend to their crops.

There was only enough water for one bath a week per family, and that was in only six centimetres of water!

There were no television sets, only radios (called the wireless). Every afternoon children waited eagerly for a programme called Children's Hour.

In Britain, the government gave every adult and child a gas mask. It had to be carried everywhere in case of a gas attack.

Bomb shelters started to appear in school playgrounds and back gardens. Parents volunteered to join the Home Guard, the Women's Voluntary Service and to act as air raid wardens, to help protect their local community.

The bombing of London and other big towns and cities began in 1940. Blackout curtains had to

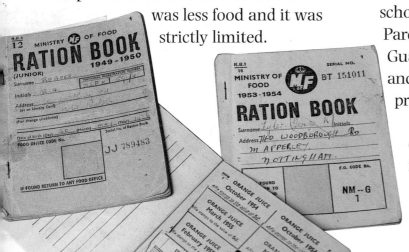

be put up at night, so that enemy aircraft flying above could not see a chink of light. When the air raid siren sounded to warn that the enemy was coming, everyone ran to the nearest shelter, even during school lessons or at night. In the morning, people often could not recognise the town where they lived because many of the buildings had been reduced to rubble.

Children who had not been evacuated made the most of the situation, even though it was dangerous. They collected parts of aircraft or shells in the debris and looked in amazement into the huge craters left by bombs and aircraft that had gone down.

In this book you can read short biographies of four children who lived through a very unusual period of history. They lived at the same time but in different places. All their lives were changed by the war.

The children came from all over Europe and beyond.

Molly lived in Guernsey in the Channel Islands. This was the only part of Britain occupied by the German Army.

John lived in London and saw bombs fall all over the city during the Blitz.

Gloria lived in the British Crown Colony of Jamaica. Her brother fought for Britain as a pilot in the Royal Air Force.

Hella lived in Austria and she was Jewish. She had to leave her home and travel to Britain to find safety.

UNITED KINGDOM
LONDON
NETHERLANDS
GUERNSEY
GERMANY
VIENNA
FRANCE
AUSTRIA
JAMAICA
KINGSTON

3

How we know

A biography is the story of someone's life written by another person. A biographer can use many different sources of information to write the story. These are some of the sources we have used to find out about the lives of four children who lived through the Second World War.

Oral history

Lots of people who are now adults were children during the war. Many have recorded their memories of the war on tape or in writing. Some of the stories have been published in books or on websites so other people can read them. Gloria's memories were recorded by staff at the Museum of London and are kept safe in their archive for future generations to read.

Autobiographies

These are accounts people tell about their own lives. Some of them are published in books. Autobiographies show experiences from a personal point of view. Molly has written her own autobiography and published it as a book. John is writing his autobiography for his grandchildren.

A CHILD'S WAR
The German Occupation of Guernsey as seen through young eyes . . .
by Molly Bihet

Newspapers

Many libraries keep newspapers that were written during the war. They are a good source of information about the events of the war. Hella has written articles about her experiences in *The Guardian* newspaper.

Ephemera

This means items printed on paper that have only survived by chance. They include ration books, recipe books and information about blackouts and shelters issued by the government to every household. Molly's letter from Winston Churchill is an example of ephemera.

I have been deeply touched by all the messages of good will which have reached me at this time. Thank you so much for your kind thought.

Winston S. Churchill

May, 1945.

Pictures and photographs

These show what people looked like and what they did in wartime. Newspaper photographs recorded events like evacuation and air raids. John and Molly still have photographs of themselves when they were living through the war. Hella has photographs of herself in Austria before she came to Britain.

Objects

Some objects used during the war, such as old gas masks, have survived and are found in family or museum collections. In the Channel Island museums you can see many of the things that families like Molly's had to use during the German occupation.

John

John lived with his mum and dad in East Ham in London. The East end of London was bombed heavily for many months in World War II. We call this period the Blitz.

It was 31st August 1939 and war was looming. Thousands of children were leaving London in case the city was attacked. John and other children from his school in the East End were being evacuated miles and miles away to Weston-Super-Mare, in Somerset.

John's parents took him to the train station to see him off. John carried a small suitcase and a gas mask in a cardboard box. A brown label with his name and the name of his school hung from his coat. John was six years old. He had never been away from home before and didn't know who was going to look after him or where he was going to sleep that night.

Three days later war was declared. Londoners were expecting bombs to fall straight away but it was so quiet that everyone found it hard to believe there was a war on at all. They called this time the 'phoney war'.

John was terribly homesick and didn't like being separated from his family. Just before Christmas, much to his relief, John's dad came to fetch him back home.

John's mum and dad became air raid wardens

Soon after Christmas, John woke one morning to see a large, strange-looking package in the front garden of his house. John and his family opened it up to find that inside there were pieces of corrugated steel for making a bomb shelter, called an Anderson shelter.

John and his dad set to work building their shelter. They dug a hole a metre deep in the garden. John held the metal pieces up while his dad bolted them together. It was quite tiny inside, with room for five narrow bunk beds – just enough space for John's family and for some neighbours.

John watched as his dad ran an electric lead from the house into the shelter to provide some lighting. He also put in two paraffin lamps in case the electricity was cut off, and some bottles of drinking water. Just outside the entrance he put buckets of sand and water and a stirrup pump so that if any small bombs fell nearby, he would be able to put out the fires.

The first bombing raid came on 7th September 1940, and every night from then on there were more. John remembers his mum putting up the blackout curtains, so that no lights from the house would be seen by aircraft flying overhead. Then, the grown-ups would sit round their radio set and wait for the signal. When the wireless began to crackle, they knew German bombers were on their way. Sometimes the rumble of the planes would make the lights dim or even go out altogether.

Air raid wardens kept watch for enemy planes and when they came into view, sounded the air raid siren for everyone to take cover. John's mum would hustle him out of bed, wrap an eiderdown round him and hurry him into the shelter at the end of the garden. There, John and his parents listened to the deep throbbing sound of German aircraft approaching from the distance, the whistle of bombs as they fell and the explosions, as the bombs hit their targets.

The Germans used several different sorts of bomb and John made it his business to know them all. Incendiaries were small bombs which fell in bundles. Landmines were dropped by parachute and exploded before they hit the ground. Delayed action bombs did not explode until the aircraft had left the scene, and some bombs did not explode at all. They just buried themselves at the bottom of

Children still played in streets where houses had been bombed.

the bomb
craters they
created when
they hit the ground.

One night in the shelter
John and his family felt a particularly
heavy ground shake. A bomb had dropped
out of the sky and landed outside their front
door! The whole family went round to John's
grandparents' house while men from the bomb
disposal unit came to take the bomb apart. Fortunately
it was a 'dud', meaning it hadn't blown up because it was
broken. It had hit the house and cracked some of the
brickwork, but it could have been much, much worse.

Once during an air raid, John popped his head out of the shelter to see what was happening. Even though it was daylight, he saw the sky streaked with smoke from burning buildings and to the south, over the London docks, the sky was full of aircraft. The German planes were flying in formation, and British planes were flying between them, shooting them whenever they could. Parachutes dotted the sky as airmen from both sides escaped from their burning planes. It was a sight he would never forget.

Early in 1941, John's dad joined the Royal Air Force, so John and his mum had to leave home and move to the town nearest to his dad's air base. They moved often over the next three years as John's dad moved from air base to air base. Every time they moved, John went to a new school. From time to time they went back to East Ham for a few weeks. On one of their visits home the Germans started using a new weapon, called the doodlebug.

The doodlebug was a flying bomb, which was launched miles away on the continent, and flew to England on its own. Everyone dreaded the moment when the hum of this bomb's engine stopped because this told them that it was about to fall. At that time John's mum was expecting another baby so they left London again. In 1944 John's sister Anne was born.

The family finally came home in April 1945, just a month before the Germans surrendered. There were big celebrations in London and people danced in the streets although the war was not completely over until August, when the Americans dropped two terrible atomic bombs on the Japanese cities of Hiroshima and Nagasaki. These forced the Japanese to surrender too.

One year later, in August 1946, there was a street party in East Ham to celebrate the first anniversary of the end of the war. It was a warm, sunny day. Flags and bunting seemed to appear from nowhere and were hung across the street. Tables and chairs were carried out from every house and in the kitchens, mothers were busy preparing party food, even though there was still food rationing. After tea, there were games and sports. Everyone went home tired and happy, knowing that they were safe and the sirens would sound no more.

The doodlebug was a bomb that fell when its engines stopped.

When John grew up

In 1957 John went to work in Australia and ended up staying there. All his children and grandchildren are Australians and he is now writing his autobiography to tell them about his experiences in the Second World War.

Hella

Hella was born in Vienna, the capital of Austria. In 1938 Austria was occupied by Germany. Hella and many other Jewish children fled to England to escape persecution by Hitler's Nazis.

Hella knew that Hitler was an evil man who hated Jewish people. He introduced laws which stopped Jewish doctors and lawyers from working. He encouraged vandals to attack Jewish shops and banks. Hella was shocked when the Nazis burned books by famous Jewish authors. Every day more and more ordinary Jewish people were attacked by Hitler's special police force, called the SS. Some Jews were beaten up in the street. Others were arrested even though they had done nothing wrong. Some were taken away from their families and put into prison camps.

A Nazi soldier outside a shop. The notice says in German 'Don't buy from Jewish shops'.

Some British families knew about the awful things Hitler was doing and offered to take Jewish children into their homes. These children came to Britain from Austria and Germany on a special train called Kindertransporte, a German word meaning transport for children.

In March 1939, Hella and her mother set out for the West Bahnhof train station in Vienna. When they arrived they saw lots of children waiting with their parents on a platform next to one of the special trains. Just like Hella, each child carried one small suitcase. Most people looked sad and nervous.

Nobody really knew for sure what was going to happen. Hella waited in line with her mother. She looked up at one point to see Nazi soldiers staring at the children as they boarded the train. The soldiers looked mean and unfriendly and they did not let the parents get on to the train with their children.

The train drew out of the station. Hella felt very alone and unhappy as she waved goodbye to her mother. None of the children in that train knew if they would see their parents again.

13

Hella was miserable, but she knew she was not the only one. Other children were crying as they all began the longest journey they had ever taken.

The train made its way slowly through Austria and Germany. It seemed to go on forever. There was an excited atmosphere in the carriage when they neared Holland. Holland was a country not yet under the rule of the Nazis, and Hella and the other children could feel a bit safer once they were there.

The train stopped for a break inside the Dutch border and some kind people gave Hella and the other children fresh bread and milk. Then the train moved on to the Hook of Holland, where the children left the carriages and boarded a boat to cross the North Sea. Hella's first sight of England was the port of Harwich. From there, she took another train to London. By this time Hella was very tired and very cold. Her journey had taken almost four days. She was in a strange country with a strange language and she didn't know a single person.

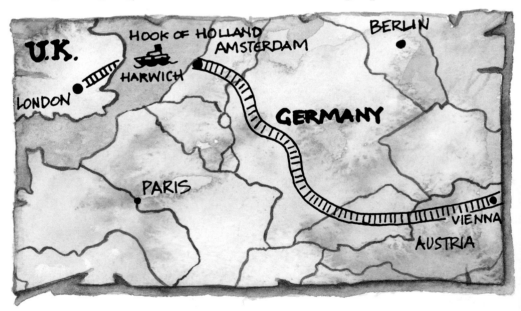

At Liverpool Street station all the children were shuffled into a large room. A group of English people was waiting there. Hella saw that they were smiling and she thought they looked friendly.

A man began to read out a list of the children's names. When Hella heard her name called out a man and a woman stepped forward to welcome her.

'Hello, we are your foster parents in England,' they said. Hella didn't know what to say, as she only knew one word in English. She decided she would try it anyway.

'Goodbye' she said. Of course she didn't really mean to say goodbye to them, but they thought it was clever of her to try to speak English.

Mr and Mrs Infield were very kind and made Hella welcome at their home in London. They only spoke a few words of German and they realised that she could not always understand what they were saying in English. It was a difficult time for Hella.

Hella went to a local school where she quickly learnt to speak enough English to talk to the teachers and the other children. At the end of the term Hella had improved so much that she passed all of her exams writing in English.

Three months after she had first arrived in England, Hella was very excited to receive a letter from her mother. She was coming to England! Some friends had found Hella's mother a job as a cook in the Lake District and she had gained permission to leave Germany. In August Hella

left her foster family to join her mother. They had become very attached to her and were sad to see her go.

Hella thought the Lake District was very beautiful. The family her mother worked for were incredibly kind and treated Hella as one of their own children. She felt lucky to have such a wonderful home.

In September 1939, four weeks after Hella arrived in the Lake District, war was declared. By then, Hella's English was so good that she had begun to forget that she had ever lived in Austria. If one of her teachers hadn't told her to continue speaking German, she would have completely forgotten her mother tongue. Hella and her mother lived on food rations, put up their blackout curtains and listened to the news about the war on the wireless just like everyone else. But because the Lake District had a small population and no factories making things for the war, there were no bombing raids. Hella contributed to the war effort by helping to grow as much food as possible on the farms and allotments.

Only one thing upset her. During the war everyone had to carry an identity card with them, wherever they went. Inside Hella's card the government had stamped the words 'ENEMY ALIEN'. Britain was at war with Austria, her home country, and so Hella was now considered the enemy as well. This sometimes made her feel uncomfortable.

When the war ended, newsreel films and newspapers showed pictures of the terrible things that the Nazis had done to the Jewish people in Europe. Hella and her mother knew how lucky they had been to escape to Britain in time and were grateful for all the help they had been given.

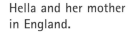
Hella and her mother in England.

When Hella grew up
After the war, Hella and her mother moved to London and became British citizens. Hella became a journalist and travelled all over the world writing stories for her newspaper. She went back to Vienna many times but, as she had left when she was a very young child, it never felt like her real home.

Molly

Molly was born in 1931 in the Channel Island of Guernsey. Molly's island was occupied by the German army in 1939.

Molly's home, Rose Villa, was close to the beach and overlooked the harbour of St. Peter Port in Guernsey. Molly lived with her mum and dad and her younger sister Joyce, as well as her grandpa and her uncle Reg.

On 3rd September 1939 Molly sat down with her family to listen to the wireless. They knew that war was brewing in Europe but it was still big news when the Prime Minister announced that Britain was officially at war with Germany. Germany seemed a long way away from their living room.

The following summer, the German army marched into France. France was so near to their island that Molly's parents began to discuss moving to England, which was further away. Some families on the island had already left.

One morning, Molly's mum woke her early. Molly looked at the clock. It was only 6 am. Her mum told her that she and Joyce were leaving the island that day. Her dad and uncle were staying. The girls had to quickly pack a few items of clothes. Their mother put gas masks round their necks as they left the house.

When the three of them got to the harbour Molly's mum was told they could not leave after all. They tried to leave three further times but, each time, they were stopped. Soon the evacuations ceased altogether.

28th June 1940 was a bright, sunny day. Molly and Joyce went down to the grocers to buy some food and as they left the shop they saw planes cruising overhead. Molly waved the cucumber she had in her hand at them. A minute later something awful happened: the planes swooped over the harbour and began to machine gun and bomb the ships moored there.

The noise of the explosions was terrifying. Molly and Joyce ran into a friend's basement nearby to take shelter. They learned the next morning how lucky they were. Thirty-four people had been killed in the bombing raid.

Two days later, German soldiers landed on the island and took control. Molly watched some of them lay dangerous mines on the beaches. Ugly concrete bunkers and barbed wire began to appear along the seashore and in the fields. New rules and regulations were posted in the newspaper and on noticeboards.

Although Molly and the islanders were not afraid all the time, they knew they were prisoners on the island and they had to do whatever the Germans said. Molly got used to seeing German soldiers walking around with daggers, guns and rifles. Some families were thrown out of their homes so the soldiers could live in them.

Across the road from Rose Villa, there was a house which held prisoners of war from many different countries. Molly watched them as they were marched off to build gun stands and even underground hospitals for the German soldiers. They wore shabby clothes and their shoes were held together with string. A few of them had only sack cloth tied around their feet instead of shoes. They looked miserable and Molly felt very sorry for them.

School life didn't change much for Molly, except that she had to learn German and some of her friends had gone to live in England. Other things changed much more. The supply of goods into Guernsey steadily dwindled. Clothes, fuel and food were in short supply.

It was very hard for everyone on the island, but they began
to find ways to get through it. Even Grandpa contributed
to the cause. One day Molly came home to find him eating
a dish of sparrows, which he had caught in a trap!

Molly and Joyce played their part as well. They invented
a new game for themselves. Everywhere they went they
took their old pram with them. Some days they filled it
with firewood they found round about. Other days they
filled it with food they scavenged from the Germans. Ships
from France came with supplies for the German soldiers
and if a few potatoes fell on the ground while they were
being unloaded, the girls picked them up and hid them in
the pram until they got home.

One day Molly felt brave and jumped up to help herself
to potatoes directly off a truck. A big, scary, red-faced
German, called Otto, came round the corner and
caught her in the act. He grabbed her and gave her
an almighty kick! She pulled herself free and ran
home as fast as she could. Molly's father was furious!
He wanted to kick Otto himself, but there
was little he and the other islanders
could do. Molly wore her bruises
with pride because she had
escaped with the potatoes
still in her pram.

Molly and Joyce became famous for their singing and dancing and they were good enough to join in the Variety shows held on the island.

By now Molly and the other islanders were praying for news that Britain would invade France, fight the Germans and make everyone free again. At first they couldn't find out any news. The occupiers had confiscated all the wireless sets on Guernsey and anyone caught using one was sent to prison. However, a few islanders broke the rules and news eventually leaked through that the war was turning in the Allies' favour.

The Finigan sisters performed in shows around the island, until June 1944 when the Germans forbade entertainment of any kind.

Then, in 1944 hundreds of British planes roared overhead. Molly and her family guessed that something important might finally be happening. They found out a few days later that Britain and the Allies had landed in Normandy in northern France. They seemed to be winning the war!

Molly was even more excited when food parcels started arriving at Christmas. They were sent by the International Red Cross, on a ship called 'Vega'.

The supplies came from New Zealand and Canada and were things Molly had not seen for a long time - sugar, butter, white flour, biscuits, jam, chocolate and much more. Molly bit into a piece of white bread for the first time in years. It was as delicious as cake! Suddenly the islanders were smiling again. The German soldiers looked tired and miserable.

On 9th May 1945, Molly and Joyce looked out to sea from the upstairs window to see British ships sailing towards the harbour. What a fantastic sight! The soldiers disembarked and all the people of Guernsey rushed out to greet them. There was no resistance from the German soldiers. Finally, the long years of occupation were over.

Molly wanted to thank Mr. Churchill for winning the war and making Guernsey free again, so she wrote him a letter. To her great surprise she received a reply. Molly, her family and all the islanders celebrated non-stop for days and days.

10, Downing Street,
Whitehall.

I have been deeply touched by all the messages of good will which have reached me at this time. Thank you so much for your kind thought.

Winston S. Churchill

May, 1945.

Molly's letter from Winston Churchill.

When Molly grew up

Molly married Andre, who was also from Guernsey. During the war he had been evacuated to Glasgow in Scotland, but his family returned to Guernsey in 1945. Today Molly and Andre live across the road from Rose Villa and run a guest house. Some former German soldiers who were stationed in Guernsey during the war have returned to the island on holiday and stayed at the guest house with their families.

Gloria

Gloria was born in the Caribbean island of Jamaica, in the West Indies. When war broke out in Europe in 1939, Jamaica was part of the British Empire and Jamaicans were British citizens.

Gloria was born in the countryside. When she was nine months old, she went to live with her wealthy aunt and uncle in Kingston, the capital of Jamaica. Gloria's aunt had no children of her own and wanted to raise Gloria as her own. Gloria's two older brothers stayed in the countryside with their parents. Gloria often went back to see them.

Gloria's aunt and uncle lived in a large, comfortable house. Her uncle owned a factory and he went to work there every day. Auntie stayed at home and looked after Gloria.

There were maids to do all the cooking and cleaning and Gloria had the best of everything. She was much more fortunate than most children in Jamaica.

When Gloria was five years old she started school. The two subjects Gloria liked best of all were mathematics and history. Jamaica was part of the British Empire, and had the same king and the same flag as Great Britain. At school, Gloria learnt all

about the kings and queens of England,
and sang patriotic songs about Britain
such as 'There will always be an England',
'Rule Britannia', and 'Land of Hope and Glory'.
Every year on 24th May, all the school children
paraded round a Union Jack to celebrate Empire Day.

One day in September 1939 Gloria, her aunt and uncle
were listening to the BBC World Service on the wireless. The
announcer told them that Britain and Germany were at war!
Later, King George VI made a special announcement to his
subjects whom he called 'my people at home and my people
across the seas'. The King asked Gloria and all Jamaicans to
stand together to defeat Hitler.

Soon after war was declared, ships from the Royal Navy
started to arrive in the port at Kingston. Gloria and her
friends watched the huge warships arrive in the harbour.
They had come to protect the merchant ships which took

sugar, cotton, coffee and bananas from the West Indies to Britain. There was a chance that the Germans might want to sink these ships so that Britain would run short of food.

Gloria and the other children did not fully understand what the fighting was about or the places where it was happening, but they wanted to help Britain to win. At Gloria's school, the head teacher gathered all the children together and told them that everyone had to do their bit for the war effort. The children donated pennies into a collecting tin in the school hall. Soon, Gloria and her classmates were told that enough money had been collected from the all the schools in Jamaica to buy a squadron of aeroplanes!

Sometimes Gloria heard Auntie and Uncle talking about the news they had read in the newspapers. Now and again the papers reported sightings of German submarines, called U-boats, off the coast. It was very frightening whenever this

happened. Gloria knew from her lessons that these submarines sank many ships with their underwater torpedoes. The grown-ups were afraid that if Britain and its Allies lost the war, Germany would occupy Jamaica and use it as a base to invade America. Gloria felt safer when the

From the shoreline, Jamaicans could sometimes see German submarines coming up for air.

British allowed the Americans to build a big army camp in the north of the island. America was going to help defend Jamaica.

Everyone did as much as they could for the war effort. Gloria helped Auntie to knit blankets, socks and woollen hats for soldiers and airmen. Lots of people collected scrap metal, which was taken to a safe port for shipment to Britain.

26

Everyday things such as old saucepans and food tins were put on the scrap pile. The pans and tins would go to Britain to be made into shells and bombs. Gloria and her family felt proud to be joining in and helping the 'mother country'.

There was no rationing in Jamaica during the war, but there were shortages. People could no longer get rice from South America and Gloria missed her favourite dish of rice and peas. Oil for lamps, which also came from abroad, was in very short supply.

However, there were lots of bananas to eat. Before the war, Jamaica grew many bananas, which were transported to Britain. During the war, supply ships from Jamaica often couldn't get past the enemy blockade in the Atlantic Ocean. While British children did not have a single banana, Jamaican children had too many!

Early in the war the British government made an appeal for young Jamaican men to join the Royal Air Force.

Boat loads of bananas could not cross the ocean to Britain.

It was a shock for Gloria when her brother Melbourne decided to go. It was a big opportunity for him to travel abroad so he put on his new uniform, kissed Gloria goodbye and sailed off in a troop ship to England. Although he wrote home often, the family did not see him for four years.

In the middle of the war, Gloria's life changed completely. Her aunt suddenly died and her real parents sent for her to go back and live with them. She was needed to help with her five younger brothers and sisters and to do chores on her parents' farm. She had to go to a new school where the classes were much larger than in her school in Kingston.

Gloria longed to go back to the city, where everything was familiar. But she knew the war meant sacrifice and change for everyone.

In 1945 the news came over the wireless that war in Europe had ended and, a few months later, the war against Japan ended too. Everyone was happy and there were Victory parades through the streets of Kingston. Gloria wished she could have been there.

When Gloria grew up

In 1955, Gloria emigrated to Britain, where she has lived ever since. She went to college in London and has had many different jobs. She has been back to Jamaica on holiday to look at the places where she lived as a child. She is often invited into schools to tell children about life in Jamaica.

Time line

International events

Nazi party comes to power led by Adolf Hitler.

1933

Germans occupy Austria and Czechoslovakia.

Kristallnacht (the night of broken glass): Hitler's soldiers set fire to synagogues, ransack Jewish shops and arrest 30,000 Jews.

First Kindertransporte (Children's trains) organised to rescue Jewish children.

1938

Germans occupy Poland.

Britain declares war on Germany (3rd September).

1939

Germans occupy Belgium, Holland and France.

Winston Churchill becomes Prime Minister (May).

British army evacuated from beaches at Dunkirk (June).

Germans occupy the Channel Islands (June).

Battle of Britain (July-October).

The Blitz: German aircraft bomb London and other large British cities (September 1940 - May 1941).

1940

USA enters the war after Japanese attack on Pearl Harbour (7th December).

Clothes rationed in Britain.

1941

Italy surrenders.

1943

D day: British, American and Canadian armies land in northern France (June).

Sightings of U-boats in Atlantic/Caribbean.

Paris liberated (August).

1944

Channel Islands liberated (May).

VE Day: Germany surrenders and the war in Europe ends (May).

USA drops atomic bombs on Hiroshima and Nagasaki. Over 100,000 Japanese people are killed.

VJ Day: Japan surrenders and the war in the Far East ends (August). Blockade of ships in the Atlantic Ocean.

1945

Victory celebrations.

1946

Personal events

Hella is put on the Kindertransporte to England (March).

John is evacuated to Weston-super-Mare (September).

Gloria's class helps to raise money to buy an RAF Spitfire.

John and his family live through the London Blitz.

Molly witnesses German occupation of Guernsey.

Gloria's brother joins the RAF.

Hella helps to grow vegetables in the Lake District.

John's father joins the RAF and his family leaves London.

John's family return to London and see doodlebug bombs.

Molly's family receive food parcels from a Red Cross ship which lands in Guernsey (December).

Molly writes to Winston Churchill to thank him for winning the war and receives a letter in return.

John's family go to a street party to celebrate the first anniversary of the end of the war.

How to find out more

Visit the local history collection in your library

Most libraries have collections of old newspapers. Read how they reported the war. Look closely at the photographs and advertisements to see the differences in the way people lived then compared to how they live now.

Visit a museum

Go to your local museum and see if it has a section on the war. Find out how it affected the people in your area.

Look at the school log book

If your school was built before 1939, there will be a record of wartime events in the school Log Book. Log Books are either kept in schools or in the Local Record Office at the Borough or County Hall.

War memorial

Find your nearest war memorial. The names of local people killed in active service are inscribed there. Civilians killed by bombs are not listed. A service of remembrance for the dead is held on November 11 every year.

Log on

Find out more about the war on these websites.
www.museumoflondon.org.uk/MOLsite/exhibits/blitz/intro.html
Find out what it was like to live during the Blitz.
www.iwm.org.uk
Go to the Imperial War Museum site to explore the Cabinet War Rooms where Winston Churchill planned Britain's war efforts, and to read the war stories of people all around the world.
www2.warnerbros.com/intothearmsofstrangers
Read about the lives of several Kindertransporte children. This site includes plenty of interesting photographs.

Things to do

Write about your life

Write part of your autobiography. Illustrate it with drawings or photographs of you and the other people in your life. Add pictures of where you have lived and of important events that have happened since you were born. Include a map and a time line.

Write a war biography

Can anyone in your family tell you about life in the Second World War? If so, ask them where they lived, what jobs their parents did and what they can remember about life then. They may even have some old photographs.

Imagine a conversation

Compare the experiences of two of the children in this book. Make up a conversation they might have had if they had met.

Become a journalist

Imagine you are a journalist during the Blitz. Write an account for a local newspaper describing a bomb attack you have just witnessed.

Make a plaque

Write an inscription that could be put up in Guernsey which tells visitors what happened there when the Germans occupied the Channel Islands.

Write a letter

Imagine you are an evacuee or a Jewish child. You have been separated from your parents. Write a letter to them explaining what is happening to you and how you feel. Then write a letter from them to you.

Book list

The non-fiction and fiction books below give an insight into life during the Second World War.
Nina Bawden, *Carrie's War*, Puffin Books
Molly Bihet, *A Child's War* (www.achildswar.co.uk)
Michael Foreman, *War Boy*, Puffin
Juliet Gardiner, *The 1940s House*, Channel 4 Books
Judith Kerr, *When Hitler stole Pink Rabbit*, Puffin
Linda Newbery, *Blitz Boys*, A&C Black
Marilyn Tolhurst, *Home in the Blitz*, A&C Black
Robert Westall, *Children of the Blitz*, Macmillan
Robert Westall, *The Machine Gunners*, Macmillan

Places to visit

The Imperial War Museum, London (0870 4443852)
Visit this museum and find out about people's experiences during the Second World War, both at home and on the battlefield.

The Imperial War Museum, Duxford, Cambridgeshire (01223 835000)
A former Battle of Britain aerodrome where you can see historic aircraft, tanks and military vehicles that were used in the war.

The Museum of London (0207 6003699)
Includes a special display about the London Blitz.

The Underground Hospital, Jersey (01534 863442)
This vast underground hospital was built by prisoners of war on German orders. The site has been restored and is now open to the public.

The Jewish Museum, London (0208 3491143)
The museum includes an exhibition about the children of the Kindertransporte.

Acknowledgements

Many thanks to Rory O'Connell at the Museum of London for his help. Many thanks also to John Benning, Molly Bihet, Hella Pick and Gloria Williams for their stories and for the personal photographs they have allowed us to use in the book.

Photographs: Maggie Murray: 2t, 5t, 21; Tim Thompson/ CORBIS: 3, 24; Museum of London: 4t; Bettmann/CORBIS: 5b, 11, 26; CORBIS: 12; Getty Images/Hulton Archive: 8, 27

Index

Reprinted 2009
This edition published 2007
First published 2003 by
A & C Black Publishers Limited
36 Soho Square, London W1D 3QY
www.acblack.com

ISBN 978-0-7136-8828-3

Copyright text © Sallie Purkis, 2003
Copyright illustrations © Duncan Smith, 2003

A CIP record for this book is available from the British Library.

Printed in Singapore by Tien Wah Press (Pte) Ltd

This book is produced using paper that is made from wood grown in managed, sustainable forests. It is natural, renewable and recyclable. The logging and manufacturing processes conform to the environmental regulations of the country of origin.